W9-BOA-881

SWEET PERSUASION

5/20/11

To Tom,

Master of
Sweet Persuasion—

PAUL KARASIK

SWEET PERSUASION

The Illustrated Guide to Closing the Sale

The Business Institute

Published by Bureau of Business Practice
Simon & Schuster

Copyright MCMXM by Paul Karasik
All rights reserved. This book may not be
reproduced in whole or in part in any
manner without permission from the author,
except for brief quotations in critical
articles or reviews. Write to The
Business Institute, 899 Boulevard East,
Weehawken, N.J. 07087.

Library of Congress Catalog Number: 89-082534
ISBN-0-9625403-3-1
Manufactured in the U.S.A.

To My Parents
Nat and Leah Karasik
With Love and Gratitude

Acknowledgements

Countless salespeople have contributed
to my knowledge of the art of closing the
sale, and through the years I have had the
good fortune to experience truly great
leaders who have inspired me to provide
others with the tools for success.

My family, particularly Marilyn and
Fred Portnoy has encouraged and
supported my career and this book.
Thanks also to my friends Moss Jacobs,
Saul Ellenbogen, Alan Gompers, Lynne
Lindahl, and Tanha.

A special thanks to illustrator
Jo Ann Goldsmith and my editor and
dearest friend Gary Karasik.

Preface

Selling represents the most
readily available opportunity for an
individual to achieve unlimited
success. The concepts, strategies,
and techniques contained within
can be applied to any interaction
in which you would like to influence
or motivate the actions of others.

This book is dedicated to those who
seek to master this art.

Paul Karasik

Contents

Introduction

First there was the Hard Sell.
Then there was the Soft Sell.
Now there is *Sweet Persuasion.*

Do you want to make more money?
Do you want to close more sales?
Would you like to know how to overcome
objections?
Do you want to enjoy selling?
Is selling a source of frustration?
If you answer **YES** to any of the above
questions this book is for you!

If you are a professional salesperson,
if your success depends on your ability
to influence others, this could be the
most important book you will ever read.

Chapter One

What is Sweet Persuasion?

Sweet Persuasion is inducing someone to take action that will produce positive results for *both of you.*

Sweet Persuasion feels good.

This system of selling is for you if you understand that the journey is as important as the destination.

Sweet Persuasion feels good.

Selling is creating.
You begin with energy and something to sell.
You create friendship.
You create satisfaction.
You create profit.
You create a relationship
where there was none.

Selling is creating.
Your selling style should flow:
Rhythm, harmony, melody.

When I was a child, I asked my father,
a successful salesman,
what I needed to become a great salesperson.
Without hesitation he said,
"You've got to believe
100% in yourself,
100% in your organization, and
100% in your product.

When you go out the door in the morning,
sell yourself,
sell your organization,
sell your product.
And sell them in that order.

You'll never become a great salesperson
unless you are 100%."

Chapter Two

What Makes People Tick?

Human nature is simple:

Most people spend the greater part
of each day thinking about themselves.
Most people want to get more
of what they want or need.

All people want more
Recognition
Money
Love
Satisfaction
Security
Health
Beauty
Peace-of-mind
Joy
Intimacy
Status
Success
Happiness
Sex
Etc.

If you possess the ability
to determine exactly
what the prospect wants or needs
and are able to provide it,
you will close the sale.

You will close the sale
when the prospect perceives
the value of what you are selling
outweighs
the value of the money the prospect has.

Everyone is listening
to the same radio station.

What's In It For Me?

Everything you do,
everything you say,
must be geared
to answering this question.

"It is one of the most
beautiful compensations of this life,
that no man can sincerely
try to help another
without helping himself."

Emerson

Take an interest in the needs of others,

and they'll take an interest in you.

It's a natural law:
You receive as much as you give.

Adopt an attitude of service.
It will feel good.
Adopt an attitude of service.
You'll make lots of money.

Altruism is selfish.

Chapter Three

How to Stay Motivated

When you need motivation, answer this:
What's in it for me if I earn more money
and am more successful as a salesperson?

1. _____

2. _____

3. _____

4. _____

5. _____

6. _____

7. _____

8. _____

9. _____

10. _____

If you can't answer this question, give this
book to someone who is hungry for success.

Motivation is not a matter of will-power.
Motivation is a matter of want-power.

Take a moment.
Close your eyes.
Recall a time you achieved selling success.
Recall how you felt.

This feeling is your *Personal Success Factor.*

Stay hungry for this feeling.
Stay hungry for this success.
Super closers are always Super Hungry.

When you need motivation,
focus on this feeling.
When you are tired,
focus on this feeling.
When you are in a slump,
focus on this feeling.
When you need
to overcome the fear of rejection,
focus on this feeling.

If you *focus on this feeling,*
SUCCESS IS GUARANTEED.

Chapter Four

Why Johnny Cant Sel

Do you know how children learn?
The same way you do:
By example.

If you want to be a closer,
look at a salesperson who is a closer.
Do exactly what that person does.
You can be a closer too.

If you want to be a winner,
look at a salesperson who is a winner.
Do exactly what that person does.
You can be a winner too.

Look around. Find a model of excellence.
When you find a great salesperson,
a great closer,
spend time with this person.
You will learn, quickly and easily.
You will become a great closer too.

As a young man I possessed considerable
talent as a basketball player. In fact, in
my neighborhood, I was considered one of the
best players.

Up on the hill in back of the high school,
the older, more experienced
players could be found.

Although it felt good to be the local hero,
it was not until I began to play basketball
up on the hill
that my performance really improved.

Go up on the hill.
Play with those who are better than yourself.
Being smart is knowing
that there are things you don't know.
And always say, "Thank you."
Humility pays dividends.

Who is the best salesperson
you have ever met?

Be specific: _____

List the traits or qualities
    that contribute to this person's success:

1. _____

2. _____

3. _____

4. _____

5. _____

Check the one you believe is most important.

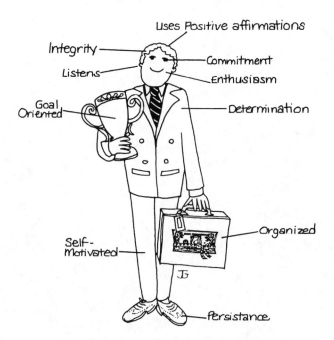

The Anatomy of Super Persuasion

SUCCESS LEAVES CLUES

Chapter Five

Why Johnny Can Sell

My first selling experience occurred when I
was eight years old. A boy in our class
suffered from cerebral palsy. My friends
and I decided to raise funds for the United
Cerebral Palsy Association with a puppet show.

We made the puppets, wrote the script, and
then sold the tickets door-to-door. As we
would approach each door I would think to
myself, "What an adventure this is!"

Sometimes we would be invited in for milk
and cookies and sometimes the door would
close quickly on us. We knocked on lots of
doors. We sold lots of five-cent tickets.
We raised over twenty dollars. Our
hometown paper wrote a story about us.

We were persistent, committed,
enthusiastic, and confident.

"Nothing in the world can take the place
of persistence.
Talent will not;
nothing is more common than
unsuccessful men with talent.
Genius will not; unrewarded genius is
almost a proverb.
Education will not; the world is full
of educated derelicts.
Persistence and determination
are alone supreme."

Calvin Coolidge

"Until one is committed, there is hesitancy,
the chance to draw back, always
ineffectiveness. Concerning all acts of
initiative (and creation) there exists one
elementary truth, the ignorance of which
kills countless ideas and splendid plans:
That the moment one definitely commits
oneself, then Providence moves too.

All sorts of things occur to help one
that would never other wise occurred. A
whole stream of events issues from the
decision, raising in one's favor all manner
of unforseen incidents and meetings and
material assistance, which no man could have
dreamt would have come his way. I have
learned a deep respect for one of Goethe's
couplets: 'What ever you can do or dream you
can, begin it. Boldness has genius, power
andmagic in it.' "

> *D.H. Murray*
> "Scottish Himalayan Expedition"

Enthusiasm is infectious.
Nobody else will get excited about what
you're selling,
unless you do.
Enthusiasm will ignite the fire
under the prospect.
You've got to strike the match.

Spectators are enthusiastic
for the day of the game.
Players are enthusiastic
for days of the season.
Champions are enthusiastic
for all the days of their lives.

It is not possible to always feel confident.
It is absolutely essential to always
exhibit confidence.

Get in the habit of exhibiting confidence.
Something magical will happen.
You will feel confident.

When you feel confident you have faith.
Faith is action in the face of doubt.

Exhibit confidence in the face of doubt.

Six Rules for Exhibiting Confidence
1. Smile
2. Wear the best clothing you can afford.
3. Look your prospect in the eyes.
4. Stand tall.
5. Relax.
6. Speak with strength in your voice.

Chapter Six

Don't Blow It on the Small Stuff

Be prepared.
Do your homework.
It is often the case,
the sale has been won or lost before
the first words have been spoken.

Here is the small stuff you must know.

1) Your personal strengths.
2) Your personal weaknesses.
3) Your organization.
4) Your product or service.
5) Your prospect.
6) Your prospect's organization.
7) Your competition.
8) Your objective for each encounter.
9) Your personal purpose for selling.

Knowledge is power,
Whoever knows more will maintain control.

A great salesperson is
an expert,
a consultant,
an adviser,
a counselor,
a guide,
a mentor,
a specialist,
a coach,
a master,
an ace,
an authority,
an educator,
a champion.

Great salespeople are not born,
they are dedicated to greatness.

Chapter Seven

How to Sell Yourself Every Time

Try this. Next time you are with an infant, look into its eyes and smile. In a soft, loving tone, recite the Pledge of Allegiance. How does the child react? How much of its reaction is based on the Pledge and how much on the way you said it?

The facts are well-documented. All studies, including one by Dr. Albert Mehrabian of the University of Southern California, conclude that people form opinions and react to you on the basis of three modalities: visual, vocal, and verbal.

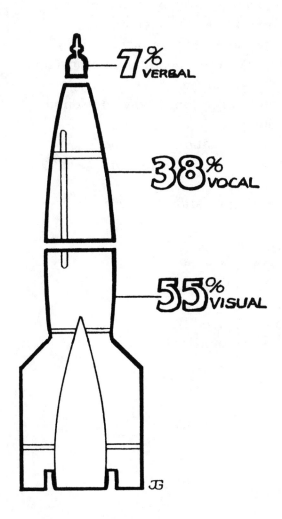

Visual is nonverbal communication —
how you look when you communicate.
Visual communication includes
facial expression, eye contact, clothing,
grooming, gestures, posture, and movement.

Vocal communication is how you sound
when you speak.
Vocal communication includes
volume, expression, clarity, and speed.

Verbal communication is words.

If you improve your
visual, vocal, and verbal
communication skills,
you will close more sales.

Chapter Eight

Closing the Sale First

Closing a sale is a process, not an event.
The Close begins when you open.

You don't need to know 1001 tricky
closing techniques.

Closing the sale is a natural
by-product of a successful relationship.

Focus on creating
successful relationships.

People buy from their friends.

Master the art of making friends.
You'll close more sales.
Master the art of making friends.
You'll eliminate the unspoken objection:
"I don't trust you."

One of my dearest friends is a lady
named Almeida. She came to live in
America from a small country in West
Africa. Almeida is a quiet woman of
few but well-chosen words. She has
a magical, powerful effect on everyone
who meets her.

Once she was my guest at a party.
She spent just a few minutes speaking
to a variety of people. Later, one by
one, I encountered many of the people
who attended the party. Almost always,
the first question they would ask
is, "How is Almeida?"

I asked Almeida, "Why do you have such
a magnetic effect on people?" She
replied, "Paul, it is my belief every
person I meet has something to teach me
and therefore I treat them with honor
and respect."

There is a sales adage:
"Give something for free."
Some salespeople give pens.
Some give a free 30-day supply.
Others give a free consultation.

You possess an unlimited supply of
one of life's most priceless treasures.
Money can't buy it.

Everyone wants it.
Everyone needs it.

Give it away.
You'll make lots of friends.
You'll close lots of sales.

Use the Four C's:
Conversation.
Common ground.
Care.
Compliments.

Conversation based upon common ground will
show that you care. Don't forget a few
sincere compliments.

Chapter Nine

The Answer Is Contained Within The Question

Play Sherlock Holmes.

The Three Most Important Selling Skills:
Knowing how to ask smart questions.
Knowing how to listen.
Knowing how to present the right answers.

Maintain control at all times.
Give up control, and you give up the sale.
Maintain control with questions.

You might start with,
Do you mind if I ask you a few questions?

Then,
May I take a few notes?

(The mind is for thinking;
the pen is for remembering.)

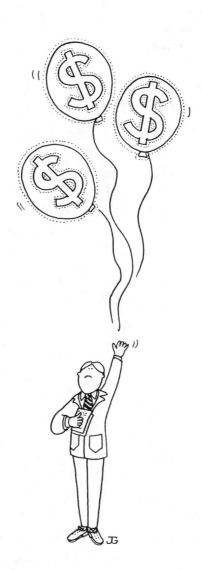

First they're suspects,
then they're prospects.

Ask questions to qualify the prospect.

Ask questions to uncover needs.

What problems can you solve?
What benefits can you provide?

If you discover a difficulty or discomfort,
don't be afraid to "gently touch the hurt."
You will confirm the need to take the
positive action you are prescribing.

The road to the big yes
is paved with lots of little questions
to which the answers are yes.
Get lots of little yeses.

Don't forget the big question:
Ask for the order.

After you ask for the order,
zip the lip.

You will be amazed at what happens.

Chapter Ten

Are You Listening?

Consider this: Your health aside,
your happiness will be determined by your
relationships with other people.
Life without successful relationships is a
shell. Similarly, if your life is
filled with loving connections with
friends and family and with harmonious
associations with colleagues and clients,
you have achieved the greater part of
success.

Your ability to communicate effectively
will dictate the quality of your
relationships.

My mother was born in Czechoslovakia.
In 1939, her parents decided to send her
and her sister on a visit to America.
It was to be the last time she would see
her parents and the rest of her family.
Hitler invaded her country shortly after
she left. My mother loved her new
homeland. She dedicated herself to becoming
a "real" American.

She learned to speak perfect English
with crystal clarity and distinct pride.

She taught me the two simple truths:
The first is, "Speak loudly and clearly if
you expect people to listen."
The second is, "Learn to
get along with people."

I have discovered my mother's two simple admonitions are among life's most profound challenges. They are also inseparable.

I have since learned a corollary to my mother's teachings: If you want people to listen, you must first listen to them.

Listening is not simply a courtesy. It is the most overlooked talent of all great salespeople.

Selling is 80% listening and 20% speaking.

Chances are if you are speaking more than
20% of time, you're probably
losing the sale.

It is more important for you to become an
interested person
than an interesting person.

The elegance of your own silence
will pay handsome dividends.

Prepare to listen:
KEEP QUIET.
DON'T TALK.
SHUT UP.

Listen visually:
Read your prospect. What do his or her
clothing, grooming, body language, and
eye contact say to you?

Listen vocally:
How your prospect sounds will
reveal unspoken feelings.

Listen verbally:
What is the content of what your prospect
is saying?

After listening,
match your visual, vocal, and verbal style
to that of the prospect.

You will create instant rapport.
You will create more sales success.

People like people like themselves.

Chapter Eleven

How to Deliver a Perfect Presentation

The professional salesperson
identifies the wants and needs of the
prospect, then determines which
benefits he or she will sell.

Professional salespeople do not sell
features.
Professional salespeople sell
benefits.

Professional salespeople do not sell
products or services.
Professional salespeople sell
benefits.

Professional salespeople sell only those
benefits
that match the wants and needs
they have identified.

People buy for emotional reasons, then justify their decision with logic.

You must create a presentation that arouses the prospect's emotions.

Your presentation should create an emotional attachment to your product.

How creative are you?
Employ words that excite the senses.
Have your presentation paint pictures.
Allow the prospect to
see, feel, hear, smell, and touch the
benefits.

Chapter Twelve

How to Overcome Objections

The only objection you can't handle
is the one you don't hear.
Become an
Objection Hound.

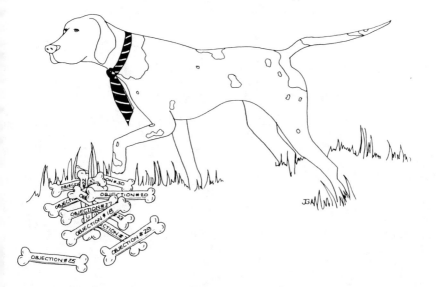

Create rapport.
Make friends.

You will eliminate the prime objection:
fear.
All other objections are secondary.

You need not fear secondary objections.
They are normal and natural.

They are good signs.
They are requests for more information.
They are details you must negotiate.
They mean that your prospect is involved.

You will always hear the same secondary objections.

The secret to handling them is to memorize your answers in advance.

Bring them out into the open.
Give them AIR.

96

Acknowledge them.

Never argue.
Show concern and understanding.
Honor the dignity of the prospect.

Isolate them.

Identify the obstacle.
What are its dimensions?

Respond to them.

Secondary objections are questions.
Answer them with benefits.

The most common objection is price.
Never attempt to overcome the
"Price Objection" with price.
There will always be someone
who can underprice you.

Sell value.
Sell service.
Sell benefits.

Don't sell price.

Sell Yourself

You will eradicate the competition.

Chapter Thirteen

Now, Shake the Money Tree

Everytime you close a sale,
you have created opportunities.

In sales, the close is not the end.
It is the beginning.
A completed sale is a seed.
Watch your business grow.

Make your clients your friends.
Friends help friends.
Most career opportunities occur
through networking.
Each person you know
knows 250 people
who know 250 people
who know 250 people
and so on.

Work your net:
Call existing clients regularly.
It costs 1/10 as much to keep a client
as to make a new one.

Networking works.
Keep your net working.

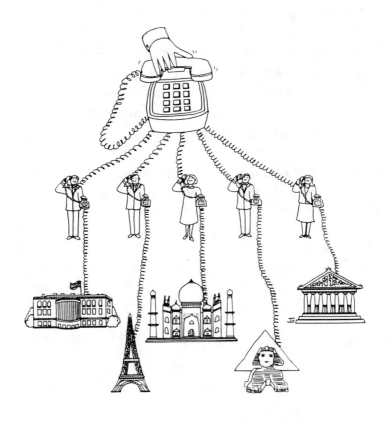

Chapter Fourteen

How to Achieve Your Goals

In college, I secretly admired certain young ladies and often felt that they were attracted to me. Yet I rarely dated. Many weekends I sat home alone.

In my class there was a young man named Harvey Langston. Harvey was of average intelligence, had no athletic ability, and was not considered handsome. What Harvey had were frequent, attractive dates.

One day out of sheer frustration I asked, "How do you do it?" He replied, "If you ask enough of them enough times . . . ."

Sales is a game of simple mathematics.
1) Write down your financial goal.
2) Divide by your average commission.
This is the number of sales you must close.
3) Determine how many contacts or
presentations, on average, it takes for
each close.
4) Multiply the answer to Question 3 times
the answer to Question 2.
5) Now you know you know exactly how many
No's you need to achieve your goal.

Learn to love No's.
It takes lots of No's to get to Yes.
Each No gets you closer to Yes.

(Although success requires failure,
keep it at a minimum.)

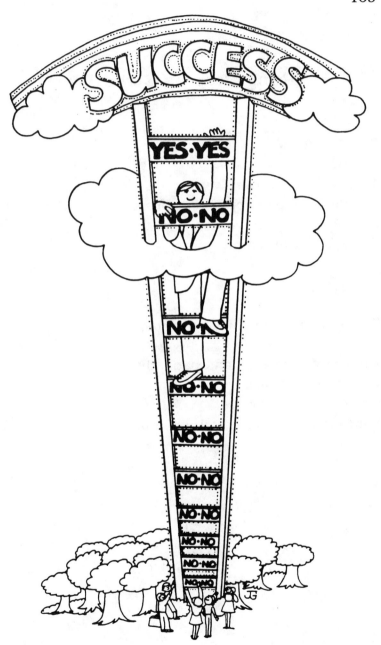

Chapter Fifteen
Making Dreams Come True

FIRST DREAM

Treasure your dreams.
They are the product of your heart,
the source of your passion,
the food of your spirit.

If you dream magnificent dreams,
set realistic goals,
and proceed steadily and patiently,
you will experience
the thrill of victory.
Your life will be filled with triumph.

THEN VISUALIZE AND AFFIRM YOUR SUCCESS

Visualizing is a process as old as mankind.

"The greatest discovery of our age has been that we, by changing the inner aspects of our thinking, can change the outer aspects of our lives."

William James

My buddy Bob uses visualizations
and affirmations effectively.
He says,
"There's a cloud over my head."
And there is.
The question is,
Are you aware of what you visualize?
Are you using POSITIVE visualizations and
affirmations?

Be positive.
Visualize your success.
See it, hear it, smell it, feel it.
Draw pictures of it;
make up songs about it.
Experience it.

Imagine that you have already
achieved it.

Be sure to visualize
successful outcomes to your sales calls.

115

Top Ten Sales Affirmations

1. I set realistic, measurable goals.
2. My first goal is to make friends and establish trust.
3. I believe in myself, my organization, and my products and services.
4. I take an interest in others, and they take an interest in me.
5. I actively listen to the prospect's visual, vocal, and verbal communication.

6. I am conscious of my visual, vocal, and verbal presentation and continually seek to improve them.

7. I treat every prospect with respect and dignity.

8. I am not afraid of being told "no" and understand that failure is a necessary component of my success.

9. I nourish myself physically, mentally, emotionally, and spiritually.

10. I use positive thought, affirmations, and visualizations to make my dreams a reality.

ALWAYS BE YOURSELF

Can you imagine a world with only
one kind of restaurant to choose from?

Or one kind of music?
Or one kind of art?
Or one kind of automobile?
Or one kind of selling style?

You are unique.

Celebrate your uniqueness.
Emulate, don't imitate.
Identify the ingredients of greatness,

Create your own recipe.

Before you know it,
people will try to imitate you.
That's quite a compliment.
(But they'll never be great until they
create their own recipe.)

Chapter Sixteen

My Wish For You

I wish for you peace of mind,
      because joy abides here.
I wish for you a healthy body, for without it
      it is impossible to enjoy
      even the most simple pleasures of life.
I wish for you to be gentle and loving to
      yourself, celebrate your strengths, and
      be patient with yourself in areas you
      are growing and learning.
I wish for you to trust your inner voice;
      this is the source of your wisdom.
      It is never wrong.
I wish for you to make the child within you
      your best friend: council that child
      when it is frightened; let it out to play
      when it is safe; and always love it
      unconditionally.
I wish for you to treasure your sense of
      humor; your ability to laugh and smile
      is one of the true measures of your
      success in living.

I wish for you to invest your time and energy
in your relationships; these are the
sparkling jewels of your life.
I wish for you to continue to open your heart;
this above all else will make this world
a better place to live.
There is a song within you.
full of hope and joy and peace
and love.
It is a song only you can sing.
I wish for you to sing your song;
sing it out,
and all the world will sing along.

Epilogue

Curiosity breeds aliveness.
Openness allows for unlimited possibilities.
Creativity is natural for the receptive mind.

Maintain an attitude of being teachable.
Invest in your education.
Your success is unlimited.

Great minds know what they don't know.

"To laugh is to risk appearing the fool.
To weep is to risk appearing sentimental.
To reach out to another
    is to risk involvement.
To expose your feelings
    is to risk exposing yourself to pain.
To place your ideas and your dreams
    before the crowd is to risk ridicule.
But risks must be taken, because the greatest
    risk in life is to risk nothing.
The person who risks nothing, does nothing,
    has nothing, and is nothing.
He may avoid suffering and sorrow,
    but he never learns to feel,
        to grow, to love, to live.
Chained by his certitudes, he is a slave.
Only the person who risks is truly free."

Anonymous

About the author

Paul Karasik is one of America's leading business consultants and lecturers. His list of Fortune 500 clients is a Who's Who of American business. An award-winning salesman who speaks from 18 years of personal experience, Karasik is President of The Business Institute, a sales and management-training company that annually trains thousands of men and woman. He is also President of the American Seminar Leaders Association.

Products and Services offered by Paul Karasik

- Motivational Programs
- Sales Training
- Audio and Video Learning Systems
- Customized Sales and Management Training

For more information on how Paul Karasik can increase your professional success, please call or write:

The Business Institute
899 Boulevard East, Suite 6A
Weehawken, New Jersey 07087

Phone (201) 864-9149 or Toll Free (800) 735-0511